Life After Physical Slavery

Yolanda explains life after physical
slavery and how it affects us today.

Yolanda Key

authorHOUSE®

AuthorHouse™
1663 Liberty Drive
Bloomington, IN 47403
www.authorhouse.com
Phone: 833-262-8899

Published by AuthorHouse 04/07/2022

ISBN: 978-1-6655-5659-0 (sc)
ISBN: 978-1-6655-5658-3 (e)

Print information available on the last page.

Any people depicted in stock imagery provided by Getty Images are models, and such images are being used for illustrative purposes only. Certain stock imagery © Getty Images.

This book is printed on acid-free paper.

This can't be all there is to life. Have you ever wondered what life would be like if you were a different nationality? Would things be the same for you or for your family? Would you undergo the same set of challenges, obstacles, and barriers? Or would things look vastly different? Although some people have pondered these questions before, many have not because 1) They are well-off and were born with a silver spoon; 2) They don't want to consider the possibility of a different life because doing so brings about endless pain and suffering; and 3) They simply don't care as long as them and their families are not harmed.

Well, I'm here to break it to those living in America specifically—if you aren't already aware—that your nationality matters beyond what you may have ever imagined. For those that may choose to deny this fact, the problem exists rather or not you choose to acknowledge it.

Contents

Acknowledgement

First and foremost, I would like to thank my Higher Power and the universe for instilling in me with the energy needed to write this book. Without the determination and perseverance, I have been so kindly given, this manuscript would not have existed. Secondly I would like to thank my husband, Kelvin Wilson, for his knowledge and understanding, and for teaching me all that he knows about the topic through his own life experiences. I would also like to thank my social media family for conversing with me, for sharing their perspectives and emotions with me, and for being part of this journey. And last but not least, I would like to thank myself and acknowledge that my dedication, hard work, research, and life experiences have made this book come to life.

Thank you.

Shattered Pieces Inside of Me

I stood still minding nature as I gathered resources to deliver back to my tribe when suddenly, a noise ripped me from my mindfulness. An uncanny sound echoed around me—something I had never heard before. At that moment, I was alone and the night was quickly approaching, so I hid from whatever it was that seemed to linger and prey in my surroundings. I laid under the debris and tried to control my breathing when a snake abruptly emerged from the bushes that were lined ahead of me. I started breathing shallow and rapid breaths, worried that if I were to move, it would strike relentlessly. I quieted myself as much as I could as it slithered away into the bushes across from me. As the moon illuminated the figure of the snake, the noise I heard earlier grew louder and closer. It was a man. Three of them. They were a different color than me—a much lighter complexion. I recognized one of the men, Sounge, he was from the Yoruba tribe. The Yoruba tribe were not friendly with our tribe, and so I continued to hide, hoping the men wouldn't see me.

It wasn't long before Sounge yelled my name from where he stood, and my frail body jumped in fear as he did. Apparently, he watched me every time I came out to this spot of the forest and knew I was hiding somewhere nearby.

I'm not sure if it was fear or just the position I was in, but my left leg became sore as it fell asleep, pins and needles making their way up to my thigh. Quietly, I assumed a more comfortable position, hoping not to alert Sounge and his men to where I was hidden away.

A branch broke in response to calculated movement, and the men's eyes darted in my direction. The two that I wasn't familiar with smiled and spoke a language I didn't recognize or understand. Again, Sounge called for me to come out and began talking nicely, as if their tribe was friendly with ours. I locked eyes with him as the dirt, rocks, and leaves crackled under his feet. He approached closer and closer and I dropped my herbs from my hands as he tugged on my arm. "I told them you would be here," he said, his voice muffled and quiet as he spoke.

Sounge turned toward the men and asked them for the gold, speaking once more in a language I didn't understand. Before I knew it, the men gathered around me and spoke loudly as they looked me over and touched me in places I had never been touched before. My breathing grew shallow and I gathered as much strength as possible, pushing the men away as they became increasingly aggressive. One of the men leaned in close, smelt me, and began rubbing me. I begged Sounge to make them stop but he only looked at me slyly and clutched the gold he held in his hand.

Knowing I was on my own, I fought all three of them with as much power as I had, but it was useless. Until mercifully, Sounge yelled, "That's enough!" Immediately, their hands fell off my body and they each took a step back.

Sounge asked for more gold, but they refused and pointed something long at him—I didn't recognize what it was. One of the men handed Sounge more gold in fear and intimidation, but one of the others slapped his hand the moment he extended it.

Then, the other man—who was quiet but more vicious than the rest—released a noise from his long stick-like object, and the man standing next to him who clutched the gold fell to the ground. He gave Sounge the gold. As Sounge turned to leave, he shouted that he would be back.

The man laid on the ground, completely still, while the others forced themselves onto me. I cried and screamed as the sky cried, cleansing me and providing me with an ounce of relief amongst the pain. From that moment on, my soul was shattered and there was no way to undo the damage that had already been done.

Interestingly enough, you'd think—like I once thought—that the people that looked like us were for us. Little did I know, they were against us, instead.

Many people from tribes adopted the mentality of doing whatever was needed to survive. However, one does not survive at the cost of hurting others. So, from that moment on, I walked feeling unclean, completely broken, and waiting to waste away. My purpose in life no longer existed. I knew that I would forever live with shattered pieces inside of me.

The Beginning

I know they can't be this naïve, especially after all that has happened. I guess these people will continue to follow the trend of hoping something or someone will come and rescue them. If no one saved Keute Kinte from getting his foot chopped off, then why would anyone save us from the bullshit that's been going on for over 1000 years?

Let me introduce myself. My name is Yolanda and I plan on walking you through the events of yesterday so you can better understand how we got to today. Living in the South is horrible. There hasn't been much change for centuries because of ignorance and fear, and most of all religion.

When I say fear, I am referring to a scenario where you were to get pummeled, kidnapped, and taken somewhere against your will. You would be afraid, too. Right? Imagine someone breaking into your home and forcing you to do things you don't want to do. Imagine helplessness.

Imagine hopelessness. Imagine hating existence. Imagine questioning God.

I have experienced racism over and over again, to the point of no return. The way my race has been treated since the beginning of time is distasteful, unethical, and immoral. Some of my people have become so accustomed to it, thinking it's simply the norm, to the point they refuse to fight against it.

I often wonder why people have become so complacent in regard to being treated unfairly and unjustly.

Over the years, I've concluded that these people are complacent because they don't want to try for change. They're tired of the process of fighting against racism and have adopted a submissive mindset, instead.

We have no choice over the color of our skin. We were born into a culture that looks down on our race and our people. We are tortured for something that is entirely out of our hands. And for what? We have no say over the living conditions we were born into, or over the family we were born into, or over the struggling environment we were born into.

The things we experience on a daily basis take a toll, although you may believe otherwise. Tell me, what would you choose? A family that is strong and full of love, or one that forces you to work like a slave just to exist?

Of course, I would choose the former. But I wouldn't choose it at the expense of hurting others.

The Jobs We Choose

We tend to believe that our choices don't hurt others, but they do. In fact, I'd argue that the professions we choose hurt others. Let me explain. Let's take a doctor as an example. A doctor studies for years to attain the profession for the money or for the intention of saving lives—or both. But does that person acknowledge the negative effects of medicine on others? Does that person acknowledge that their profession may bring more harm than good? Most don't and as a result, they expect praise in return for healing you. I mean no disrespect to a person who has chosen to be a doctor as I understand the decision stems from a society trying to survive at any and all costs.

Nurses, on the other hand, don't hold as much blame because they are only following orders, although they still chose to make that decision.

There are holistic doctors and nurses out there who have a better outlook on healing people, but still add to the harm caused through the profession as a whole. With that being said, I'm sure you're wondering, "Well, what about the firefighters? What about the paramedics?" They are under-recognized in society, although they sacrifice their lives in times of crises. Now, what about the lawyers and judges? Useless. Sure, in the society we live in, lawyers and judges are necessary in keeping society stable, but let's dissect this concept first. If the bible holds any truth, then we can question why we're judging one another instead of allowing mother nature to take its course? I'll tell you why. The punishment isn't fast or cruel enough for us. We want to be in control of one another. We want to make revenue off of one another and off of justice and punishment. You may wonder, "Then what about the murders and rapists that live among us? If we let mother nature take its course, then how can we prevent these injustices from happening?" Simple. If you do something to me, then I do something to you. Lawyers get paid to convince others about the facts and outcomes of a case, letting a jury or judge decide what is right or wrong. But what about bias? What about prejudice? Are their decisions right or fair? No! Besides we should not allow others to make decisions about moral aspects of society as these increases the number of misunderstandings. There are differing views on what is considered right and what is considered wrong. Philosophically speaking, right and wrong are subjective. There is no black and white answer—there is always a grey area when it comes to moral conclusions. Let's consider slavery as an example of this notion. They lost their lives as a result of other people's inhumane decisions. What about the people that were put in jail for crimes they didn't commit and were released 20 to 30 years later and appeased with money? Is finance a trade-off for lost time? I am going to allow you to think about it.

Society wants us to accept injustice regardless of the severity of hurt and damage it caused. And so, we're pushed into accepting unethical things just to get by, stay afloat, or stay popular or relevant. Can we survive like this? Maybe. But we must understand and acknowledge that our past has caused more harm than good for our future. We are creatures full of emotions inexplicable because we have taken mythical stories and attached them to ourselves and living arrangements, believing they are about us. And to a certain extent, they are, but not as much as we may believe. Take the story of Jesus. The letter j was not created until the late 1400s, so I really don't understand how we as individuals pray or worship something that was not created just a few 1000 of years ago when creation started way before the letter j existed. Then the point that Jesus is our lord and savior, and he is saving us from our sins so we can have eternal life as an example. Does this make you question your existence? Let's dig deeper. Why were we created to die or deteriorate? This story doesn't justify why we were born and why we have to keep changing hosts as our souls transfer from one place to another. What happens to the pain we experience?

Does it simply disintegrate? What about the bad decisions we make?

Will we ever be punished for them, or does our punishment transfer with our souls? Realistically speaking, these are questions we will never receive answers because no one that has died has come back to tell us this in living times that would believe it. We can observe the things that happen to us and around us, but we can never attach definite reasons to these happenings.

Circling back to the conversation about professions. We have police officers who fall into a category of their own. The majority of their actions are not frowned upon by most. Essentially, if all police officers did what was right for the greater good of humanity, they would be considered tolerable by the less fortunate. It is important to note that not all cops are bad, but most of them are perceived to be bad because of the actions of a handful of police officers dating back to slavery. In the era of physical slavery, the police officer profession was created to tame slaves and keep them in line, while also capturing those who ran away. It's unfortunate that an entire profession suffers as a result of individual views on one another's skin color.

Similarly, all other professions play some role in dehumanizing individuals simply because they have a specific job title. Consider correction officers and wardens in prison. I'm sure we can both agree on the notion that certain jobs were created to keep individuals in line who break the law and cause harm to others and to themselves. You might wonder, "What's wrong with that?" I'll tell you what's wrong with it. Conditioning people to do things against humanity is wrong regardless of how you spin it. What happened to asking people to do things, or letting them make the decision, exercising their own free will?

What about trading? Wouldn't this be better for humanity as a whole? Currency removed aspects of our humanity, whether we want to agree with it or not. For instance, people lose all morals and respect when it comes to currency, and some are viewed as inferior for not having it. Commercialized living has dehumanized us. We weren't sent to earth with any of these things required for survival. So why are we working so hard for things we didn't come here with? Yes, some may argue that it makes life easier, but it still isn't needed. In fact, survival has become so commercialized to the point where we don't even know what being human is anymore, and we can't survive off our own habitat.

Destroying Our Humanity

We have destroyed so many things through our lifestyles to the point where it would be impossible to find our purpose now. We've destroyed the environment, trees, forestry, clean air, and so much more. Nothing we can do to unlearn or undo this because the actions are stored in our mental memory bank. Take a step back onto reality, or have you ever thought about the cleaning and landscaping of an area. Why does this even exist if our creator created the rubbish in the first place? Just as simple as being a male or a female. We makeup ways to portray to be something that we are not, and we all are guilty of doing this even if we change our hair color or wear bras or false teeth we still are going against nature. What about women baring children or males becoming females, changing our sexual orientation because of a feeling or it could be of hurt let's not look over this, regardless of the situation or the emotion, we are still going against humanity.

Moreover, let's take a look at women as a whole. Their color, sexual orientation, and independence. I am speaking from experience when I say women are both a blessing and a curse. We are a blessing because we can grow life inside us, and a curse on our decisions. I assume this will go for males as well. I can't really express my experience as a male because I am not one, I can only assume. My grandmother always taught me you can only speak on things you have experience everything else is an assumption.

Women baring children is a beautiful thing. Don't you think? Although the process often leaves me wondering why something so magnificent hurts so much. Is it a metaphor for life itself? Is the process of creation and birth teaching us that to get something extraordinary in life, we must do things out of the ordinary? We must suffer? We must feel pain? Time after time, we may question why things happen the way they do, or why it takes things so long to work out.

Education

Education plays a big part in our downfall. We should all receive an education up to the 7th or 8th grade—nothing more and nothing less. The reason for this is experience can't be taught from a book. Experience is the best teacher, and it doesn't waste time like high school. Let me explain, from experience in life we learn from repetitive behavior or actions, unless we do something ourselves, we are the only one that can experience that knowledge to learn. True enough some people catch on to things faster than others, but they still don't feel comfortable doing it unless they experience it themselves. Even down to daycares and grade schools the teachers teach children by allowing them to do things themselves. New jobs do this as well. Education is good as well as bad, its good because of motor skills and communicating with others, and bad because most things can be learned in a shorter life span, but in a different way. Before physical slavery was abolished it was inhumane for a colored person to learn to read anything besides the bible and even then, it was a selective few that was chosen to read. Those that was chosen were the ones least likely to create uprising or to go against the agenda. If I knew then what I know now my children would have been taught very differently starting from my womb. I would be explaining to them what love is by the best of my knowledge. If I could turn back the hands of times, situations in my life would be so different.

Acceptance

In most African American families, they don't want to change because they are so accustomed to doing things the way they've always been done. Usually in our culture, we sit back, worry, and complain about things rather than make decisions that can move us toward change. Then, we go to church or bible study to feed our spirits with hope that will magically act on our free will to make a difference in our lives. However, it is crucial to acknowledge that false hope actually comes from the physical slavery era, where we hoped Jesus would save us from our unwanted pain and suffering. We didn't even consider whether Jesus had the power to save us, or why he allowed us to be captured as slaves in the first place. Similarly, what about innocent children? Why hasn't he stopped them from being murdered or raped?

I often wonder why pastors don't teach about today's societal issues. Even some schools and colleges teach you the content but make you learn by volunteering to experience what was taught. I, myself, believe some of the pastors in today's society don't have clear-cut knowledge about the things they teach, as they are still learning from experience themselves. This doesn't negate the fact that they can still offer helpful advice and direct people toward the right path. However, my point lies in the notion that we should instead be teaching the truth to people so they can learn to decide what is right and what is wrong.

We are supreme beings and are the cause and effect of everything that occurs in life. We have to put a stop to the unwanted pain that has been forced upon us, but our pride isn't allowing us to make better decisions regarding what is morally right for everyone.

We can help each other make these better decisions and can try to move forward regarding big-picture morality; however, some of our people who need help will refuse it because of selfishness and pride. They don't want to ask for help from their own people and would rather turn to the system that pushed them into oppression in the first place.

I recall these things happening often when I was in school. I had classmates that didn't know how to solve math problems but only turned to their caucasian peers for help, despite the fact that I had the answers and the highest grade in the class. Things have worked this way for as long as I can remember. I used to feel angry when I realized that the people who were like me and who were supposed to turn to me for help were instead turning to someone else.

Family is the same. They do things like this as well, For example, I have been driving trucks for 18 years now. I have family members that have beat around the bush as they tried to ask me about truck driving, claiming they wanted to do the same thing. Being the person that I am, I never withheld information from them just as I wouldn't want someone to do the same to me. So, I answered all their questions, but then heard from non-family members that they were calling me a liar about the things I shared in regard to truck driving and bashing me. I am sure situations like this happen in all black families. I call this a crab in a bucket mentality. If you put crabs in a bucket their focus is to get out instead of coming together and making a better decisions to get out of the bucket.

Similarly, I can't imagine how bad our ancestors must've felt when their own people talked bad about them to get ahead. It's a never-ending cycle and we are still engaging in these same behaviors today. We try to get promotions or raises by making reckless decisions and selling out our peers to get ahead.

Athletes also engage in this behavior, alongside rappers, singers, preachers, and government officials. They may have good intentions but they make bad decisions. They act out of an individualistic drive rather than adopting a community-based mentality. The ones that don't engage in this behavior usually have a productive and successful life, and are often remembered by others as loyal and uplifting citizens.

As African Americans, we have been hunted like dogs since we set foot in this country. We have been treated unequally until some people are fed up with the mistreatment. In response to this mistreatment, athletes have recently taken a stand to fight against the ways in which we are being gunned down and killed, beaten, and treated unequally by our oppressors. Still, there has been no tangible change. What a shame. We should be sick of this by now but some of us get caught up in the excitement of it.

The Excitement

We all get excited about things, whether they're good or bad for us. When things are exciting, we react in an energetic manner, but when we lose interest, we also lose focus on the situation and why we were excited in the first place. I assume this is what happened during slavery. Our ancestors were focused on their excitement in that moment, not realizing the repercussions of their emotions. Of course, this applies to situations that occur in today's society, as well. Living life after physical slavery is an emotional rollercoaster. Some days are good while others are bad. But no days provide can escape from things that attack our emotions.

What are some of the most exciting things that could happen to an individual? Having a baby. The people that don't get excited about this must be the ones that experienced its trials and tribulations, and don't want to repeat the experience again.

Another way we allow excitement to control our emotions is through materialistic or monetary gifts. When receiving a gift of this nature, have you ever stopped to consider what that person needed to do to give you that gift? Most of us haven't and this is because we are caught up in the excitement of receiving a gift. However, we should never be excited about materialistic things that may have caused harm to other individuals. You might be wondering, "Then what are we supposed to be excited about?" Health, strength, the greater good, the universe and all it gives us.

The issue from letting excitement control our emotions is that it becomes addictive. We have become so complacent with the results of life after physical slavery that we will go along with anything that excites us. This is related to access we have to things we did not previously have access to, loving outside of our race, owning materialistic stuff, and even eating certain foods. It may sound mediocre, but those are some of the things we did not have access to in the past.

Moreover, we should also be excited about learning new things and being able to experience new adventures in life. Still, we waste our energy on things that do not intend us any good.

The House Nigga

Women and men were raped and stripped of their dignity and pride. Life after physical slavery was not good for black people because it was as if other nations had a head start on life. Life after slavery consisted of—and still consists of—prejudice against our own people. In fact, this is common in the Black community, and it started as a result of favoritism for certain skin colors. The lighter skinned slaves were used for house work, whereas darker skinned slaved were used for work in the fields. Some slave owner men took a liking to some of the female slaves. They would rape the Black women and started picking favorites to sleep with. Then the chosen Black woman began to think she was more important than the rest of the slaves, not considering the force that was used on her, and the ways in which her body, mind, and soul were degraded.

This type of behavior made Black men upset as they were forced to share their wives with the slave master. In return, this caused the master's wife to be upset with the Black woman, as well. Clearly, slavery created things we didn't feel physically but could feel emotionally. Today, this has evolved into adultery, which of course isn't exclusive to the Black community, but has spread to all races. This adultery help uprooted the foundation of a family where there is both parents cohabitating in the household where there is love and nurture for the family as a hold. It's bad in the black community. There are too many single parent households. These single parent households help develop murderers, fornicators, pedophiles, drug users, drug dealers, disrespectful individuals to themselves as well as to others. In the black communities the mothers feel they can raise the children alone and some can, but most of the single parent household becomes a family full of voidance and survival just like it was in the physical slavery era.

White Washed Living

Why is everything that is white is deemed as superior, meaning white is good and black is bad. For example when we were coming up we were taught that the black cat was considered bad luck, and Jesus was white, and all the men on the picture of the last supper were white. Every time I looked at that picture it scared me because it seemed as if the men were looking at me to see if I was doing something wrong. I never understood why we did not have pictures of disciples or Jesus that looked like us. Now that I am older I understand the oppression better it was like master was in the household monitoring or governing us. It might sound stupid but this is the way I felt. In every Black household in America seemed to have these dumb ass pictures on the wall. Even today I have some family members that still have these pictures up, this is one of the reasons I don't even visit them because I feel they have no self-worth, and I think this is a low vibration. It's like everything was white washed, from white Tarzan that lived in the jungle of Africa, even the angels are supposed to be white. Then we have Snow white is white, the white house is white, but black people built it. Less look at all the people on the money are white men. Why are there white only things, and who thought of this any way? The reason I bring this up is, I can remember visiting the archives in Montgomery Alabama, and down town there were white only benches and water fountains displayed. I was surprised and furious at the same time because I felt things of this nature should have been destroyed years ago. The reason for them keeping it was to remind people of history. This is very negative way to remind people of history, but who am I to tell soul less people to do right by others. This is their behavior and it seems they will stick behind it. The whit washing was so bad until blacks couldn't perform at the cotton clubs, award ceremonies, or have ownership to things they created. This set black and brown people back more and more and here its 2022 we are still trying to play catch up. It's a sad reality that we are still suffering today.

Mixed Race

During the physical slavery era, many families were created because white men refused to acknowledge their offspring from raping slave women. The number of slave owners children were innumerable, and this helped develop absent parenting in Black culture. In fact, there so many fatherless children and unanticipated pain. There was an abundance of rejection, as well, in regard to not accepting one another and not taking responsibility for one's actions. If it was not for some of the slave owners falling in love with their slaves, Black people may not even be where they are today in America.

Quite a few slave owners stood up for their offspring and didn't care what society or their family thought of them. They were referred to as *nigger lovers* and were shunned by people in their family. I feel if this hadn't happened, we would still be in the physical slavery era today. After many years of research, I came across the studying of the eve gene, not that it did not exist before it always existed, I just did not care that much about history and understanding DNA like I do today. So, from my finding and listening to others experiences the eve gene can create all nationalities and it only resides in black, or brown women. Not looking over no other color of women because all women are important. I often wonder did some slave owners kill their wives for creating a black or brown child thinking that one of the slaves had intercourse with their wives? I have read books and looked at movies telling some of the stories, but hey we will never know the truth. We just have to accept the realty.

The Issues in America

The issues in America do not stem from just one culture but are rather a collective of issues from all cultures that ultimately affect everyone. Society is largely to blame for this phenomenon, as apart from racism, we have been told who to love, how to think, how to act, what to say, and what is considered normal. Is it fair for our children and our children's children to act a certain way as a result of illegitimate scare tactics? These new age children will not adopt the past mentality of, "Do as I say and not as I do." Instead, they will discover what is good and bad for them through personal experience.

Africans Accepting African Americans

Do Africans accept African Americans back into their country? Some argue that they do, while others argue that they do not. I often wondered why they wouldn't, since it was their ancestors initially that sold us or allowed our nation to be conquered. There are so many unanswered questions in our culture. In some parts of Africa, people are treated poorly and others are treated with dignity and respect. This must be the case for all areas of the world, though. Similarly, in America, status, income, and race dictate how you're treated and whether or not you're treated with respect and dignity. This is unjust, as we all hold internal and intrinsic value. We may not see the value in one another but it's there regardless, despite our societal status. It is obvious that all cultures are very timid and in fear of one another by the experience they encountered with one another. The goal is for all nations to get along, although I really don't feel this will ever happen. It's like wishing in one hand and hoping in another. It's a good thought to be looked at as an equal and not judged from a bias emotional standpoint.

The News

I see two different perspectives from the local news and social media. The news should be looked at from an informative view, but not the United States News. I feel it is used for a scare tactic to keep people on the edge of oppression and depression. When I was growing up my grandmothers and one of my aunts had to watch the news to see what was going on, but after they looked at it, they reacted funny and would get on the phone and ask family members and friends did they catch what was on the news? I can agree to be informed of the different things that is going on around us, but not to the point it scares the hell out of us. Most of the times its lies, or they gas it up to be more than it really was. I can remember one year I was following a tornado that hit land in Florida, and the news anchor was out filming it. I do not know what happened, but the real video leaked, and the anchor had a fan blowing on him and water coming down on his umbrella. After that I started researching everything on the news that was important and involved me, or people that is around me. Social Media on the other hand is different because most of the times, the videos are real time situations that happens. Don't get me wrong some of the videos are edited but when they are live you can't persuade people otherwise. Social media exposes a lot of lies we have been told about other countries, the pastors at these mega churches, adultery in the household and most of all congress. Some of us believe everything congress put out for us to believe, but most of us have stared realizing the truth. Just like in Africa and the relationship African Americans have with Africans.

The news portrays Africans as unaccepting of African Americans, but social media tells a different story in which Africans welcome us with open arms. We may be skeptical of these differing narratives because we've been tricked before and are afraid of being gullible. I know I am, especially after seeing videos that show Africans are not as friendly as they seem. We know the United States doesn't accept us, but to go to another country looking for acceptance seems scarier.

Dealing With PTSD After Physical Slavery

Post-Traumatic Stress Disorder (PTSD) plays a role in the lives of those who have been brutally harmed in the past. When discussing PTSD, many people look to the military and those who served in war. However, PTSD can be experienced by anyone who has endured or witnessed some type of trauma. In the Black community, it's unfortunate that people who experience mental illness and PTSD are categorized as "crazy." However, mental illness should not be taken lightly as it is a real sensation for those enduring it.

Interestingly enough, life after physical slavery in itself is a form of PTSD.

This is because the result of slavery is still alive and well today. You can't escape a pain when the result still lingers. However, we often aren't able to recognize the aftermath of certain events as we believe things will be okay simply because we are told that they will be. We are asked to fight in a war overseas just because the government told us or had us believe we were fighting to protect our country. This doesn't help the greater good, though, and instead causes negative effects for those living through these historical periods. Interestingly enough, the government adopts a "Do as I say and not as I do" mentality. Consider the people being raped, murdered, and slaughtered in wars our government is involved in. How does it make sense for the government to make laws against these crimes in this country, but validates and justifies their actions overseas?

We need to evaluate situations before signing up for them, especially when the result causes harm to others. The government didn't acknowledge PTSD until the 1980s, despite the fact that people have been involved in war long before then. Like many of you, I was under the impression that anything the government verified was meant to be okay. I didn't think for myself, and I didn't evaluate situations based on my own moral code. I realized that everything we do has consequences, and none of us are exempt from them.

I feel all African Americans should be treated for PTSD because we are still enduring the consequences of systemic and historical oppression. Instead, soldiers who are trained to hurt others are receiving treatment for this mental illness, and we are pushed aside as a result. I urge you to begin thinking for yourself and to begin contemplating the facts and consequences of things that are considered the norm in today's society. For example, I used to feel bad for military soldiers who experienced PTSD, but no longer do. Why? Because they are voluntarily hurting others. I know people might not agree with me in this regard and I am aware this is a controversial statement, but I came to this conclusion when I stopped believing what I was told and instead started thinking for myself.

So many of us simply go along with situations because we don't want to go against everyone else. We may believe in karma but we don't apply the concept to our own lives because we believe we can get away with some of the things we do if we aren't caught. With that being said, PTSD plays a major role in life after physical slavery because nothing is being done to fix the pain or trauma that was inflicted years prior. However, if the government acknowledges this, then it means they are acknowledging and admitting to the pain they've caused the entire Black community.

Fuck The Government

If you look around you, you'll notice that nothing is evolving. I'm sure you're tired of being sick and tired, and keeping the hope alive hasn't made any difference. It's time to act and push for change. Stop believing that miracles are going to happen and make things happen yourself. We landed on Plymouth Rock, Plymouth Rock didn't land on us. The time is now to build on our own and stop looking for someone else to lift us out of the rubble. Why are we waiting to be accepted by people that never cared if we lived or died? Is unification impossible? Will any of this ever change? Before answering any of these questions, we have to un-condition the way we were taught to follow the herd. We need to learn how to make our own. Saying, "Fuck the government" may be a hard response, but keep in mind that the government has fucked us all, that goes for white, black, brown, tan and every woman or man. We can all pave the way for a new life that can give us something more to live for. We must consider recreating our own government and stop following the same unwanted patterns. Some may believe the system works as is, but I urge you to ask who the system is working for because it sure as hell isn't working for the citizens. It isn't working for the ones trying to get by. The system is the reason for all the damage and pain we are enduring today. Before the Europeans colonized us, people got along well. Then, greed took over and forced us into making decisions that were not good for anyone but the greedy.

"We, the People of the United States, in order to form a more perfect union, establish justice, insure domestic tranquility, provide for the common defense, promote the general welfare, and secure the blessings of liberty to ourselves and our posterity, do ordain and establish this Constitution for the United States of America."

What happened to this? It may be quoted, but remember that the government adopts a "Do as I say not as I do" mentality. Note that the number one thing that is missing from the preamble above is equality for all. Name one aspect of the constitution that was written to protect all of mankind rather than a particular group of people. If this were the case, society would look very different. The laws within our country are unfair. The only solution is to create our own government and stop expecting the broken one to fix what they created.

Historically, the government treated their own people like property as they bought and sold slaves, so what makes you think they would treat us any different today? I wonder when any of this will end. When will our people think and stop acting off impulsivity? When will we realize that we can act and think on our own? We might have failed at it before but that's because we went about it the wrong way. A different approach can't hurt. Creating our own government may seem scary, but it's necessary. A lot of us frowned on Jim Crow laws and his teaching I have conclude that this really was not bad as we took it to be. The reason being keeping everything separate would allow everyone to build and cultivate better. That's just my opinion, but then I think otherwise because my grandchildren are from mixed cultures. This is when situations are on our heart instead of on our mind, and its hard to make a realistic decision, because emotions are involved. What is your take on the matter? Do you think we should keep things the way they are, or should we migrate back to keeping everyone collectively together, where we trade and build amongst ourselves? Which ever way we feel it should be, there should be a change for the greater good for all of us.

Besides I would rather try something new instead of waiting for things to change on their own.

Doing things, the old way has kept us bound and has made us stagnant to the point of accepting pain and inequality.

Blood Sweat & Tears

What do you think of when you hear someone say, "Blood, sweat, and tears?" Have you ever experienced it yourself? Can you imagine going through something so horrifying just to survive? Some of us complain about being exposed to too much sun or just a little bit of labor, but we fail to acknowledge what our ancestors experienced. Our ancestors went through so much to survive, and just from knowing they did, we should try not to complain. Imagine being in the fields all day and having to ask someone for water just to keep you from passing out or dying? I am sure some of our ancestors died from dehydration all because the over seers were mad, or someone did do their part that day in the fields. It makes my skin crawl just thinking about it. I am so glad I did not go through that when I was coming up, just hearing about it makes me appreciate the little freedom we have today. You would think things like this don't go on today, but it does, just not to this magnitude. Let me explain, some restaurants monitor what they employees consume when they are at work even to the limit of how many drinks they receive. Some employees don't receive breaks when it's the law to do so and they don't accumulate vacation pay or sick leave after so many years. This is the blood sweat and tears in society. I know some people that have worked on a job for 20 plus years and still didn't receive anything but a pat on the back. This is the result of Life After Physical Slavery because the labor laws should not have allowed this to happen.

These employees suffer from blood, sweat, and tears and are still not compensated for the work they do. Yes, businesses need to do what they can to survive and make profit, but that doesn't mean they need to overwork their employees and exploit them. We can't even afford to live or die.

Both situations cost money, time, and energy. The vast majority of us will never work like our ancestors did. The way the system has helped raise our children has made them become lazy and not desire to work or even own a business. This, however, is a result of systemic oppression against Black people and we must change that narrative because it causes us more harm than good.

Gender

What is gender? Well according to the oxford dictionary, gender is either of the two sexes male, or female. I think this is what creation ment for it to be. Although today we don't know what's a male or female unless we look at their private parts. This has become so much of a problem and society has made it a norm, in fact, it is becoming increasingly harmful, as we can't even decipher the roles of men and women. Some don't consider this an issue, but it is. Men were thought to be physically stronger than women, whereas women are mentally stronger than men. It should have never been taught this way in the first place. Society has flipped gender roles and we are going against what we were created to be. I can even speak from experience of being in the LGBQ community, I use to date the same sex, but I never felt like I wanted to be a man I knew what I was created to be I was tired of the life experiences I encountered with men. I am sure there are a lot of people in that community that felt the same way. Some will admit it and some wont. Regardless of the decisions of what gender a person tries to portray to be I just know that it takes a male and a female to create life.

Overlooking Reality

Too many of us overlook the reality of what some people go through just to survive. Life after physical slavery should not have existed in the first place. Some of the hurt that our ancestors felt was too shameful to repeat and pass on to the next generation. Reality is we can't change another person action only our own. We can only encourage people to change, but in order to do that we have to accept what we do wrong and do the necessary things to change it. For example people are still not allowing themselves to read anything but the bible, but they know and have been told that the Europeans have changed some of the literature to oppress us. The next thing is we keep participating in politics when they still won't create a protection law for black people, let's not forget about being killed by cops and we have to have a long drawn out trial to see if it's okay to punish them. We are not going to mention the inequality from the Olympics and different sports. I never understood how why we keep participating in things we were not invited too. There is so much more, we all just look over it because we want to feel we are a part of something.

Getting Therapy

Why is therapy looked over in the black community? Well for one, people are embarrassed by some of the situations they were put in, or chose to be in.

This is especially true for men during the physical slavery era, as they had increased levels of pride and did not want to admit to the things they had to endure and do to survive. In

American culture, men die incredibly young due to stress, diabetes, and heart attacks. Not to mention the killing of one another because of greed and disrespect. Black men in particular don't like to talk about their feelings, and this is a result of generational pain and trauma. Black men couldn't do anything to stop the white men from raping or beating their wives, children, or themselves. They weren't able to fight back, and were instead forced to tolerate and endure this trauma. If I were to experience even a quarter of the things our ancestors did, I'm sure I would have wished I was dead. What about you?

Mental Slavery

Now let's consider the notion of mental slavery. What is mental slavery and why is it not discussed? Are we all mentally enslaved? In my opinion, yes, we are. Every color, creed, and nationality are mentally enslaved. Rather than asking whether or not we're mentally enslaved, we should instead question *why* are we mentally enslaved? Unfortunately, there isn't a cookie-cutter answer to this question because everyone is enslaved in a different manner that is unique to their own lives, identities, and histories. We tend to measure everyone's situation collectively when certain situations have not collectively affected us.

Putting race and socioeconomic status aside, we must discuss the ways in which minorities are looked down on in society. It is unfortunate, but the reality is that we are judged and valued based on our societal status rather than our character.

Our character means nothing in today's society because the value of humans is associated with the number of zeros attached to their bank account. Some minorities think they are just as important as the next person or that they are more important than any person of color. I still can't comprehend how people can look down on others for such petty and irrelevant reasons. I do not know how many times I have walked in a department store and have been followed by the sales person. I wouldn't even think like this if I was the only person that had walked in the store but most of the times it's a caucasians that walked in with me and I am the one that was followed. I have gotten use to it, but I often ask myself, why do I have to get use to being watched when I am shopping, I have not given no one a reason to suspect me of stealing. Then you have to come to realization you can't change no one else's behavior or their mind, they have to do that themselves.

Reliving Historical Events

Dr. Claude Anderson stated something in an interview that enlightened me. Anderson shared that he never understood why there was a boycott in Alabama about sitting at the front of the bus. He made a good point, stating that it didn't matter whether you sat at the back or at the front, as long as you reached your destination in the end. We often create chaos when we don't have to. It is undeniable that white people treated Black people poorly, but I wonder whether our ancestors realized that they could've left when the opportunity presented itself. Or did they think about helping one another to travel from destination to destination? I assumed Black people were so brainwashed to the point where we didn't recognize that it was okay to help one another and stop including ourselves in things that were not meant for us. I really believe following Dr. Martin Luther king Jr. teaching was not as productive as we thought it was. We lost too many people and yet we always attach ourselves to situations that needed not as much attention. Even to the point of the right to vote and all it in tells even to going to certain schools. Today we have more successful people learning a trade than we do with degrees. We are so lost until we follow certain parties in the government.

When we consider the different parties that exist in the government, such as Democrats, Republicans, or the Independent Party, we must also acknowledge that they are each a form of separation amongst individuals. I don't claim that there is a right and a wrong party, but rather argue that we must stop including ourselves in the systems that work against us, and instead create our own. We have a lot to learn from history, but we have to first unlearn the history of lies. We all know that we cannot live in this world without one another, and the ways that we have tried to fix societal issues have not worked. It's time to take a different approach or listen to the unpopular response.

36

Get Over It

Many of us use the statement, "Get over it" to overlook the root of an issue.

Understandably, no one wants to create a problem and admit to being the source of it.

For instance, taking a life is taking a life, despite who committed the act, correct? Well it actually matters who committed the act because the punishment is related to that person's status and skin color. Undeniably, white people get less severe punishments than black people. No one is exempt from punishment except white people, not even other races and nationalities. The judges and DAs make sure of this.

Is it fair? No. Will it stop? Who knows, If we change our approach, then maybe. There have been several unjust cases that prove this statement: Sandra Bland, Tamir Rice, Trayvon Martin, Emmit Teal, and so on.

It's very difficult to grieve the loss of a loved one, but it's even harder to do so when that loved one was murdered and their killer walks free. There is no closure in this case. Some may argue that God forgives us and therefore we should forgive others; however, God puts us through trials, tribulations, and death. Regardless, the next time you hear or make the statement, "Get over it," consider how the other person feels. Consider how you would act in their position. Would you get over it?

What about scenarios where the system finds the person guilty, but they receive a lesser punishment for their crime? It's a lose-lose situation. In these cases, people begin acting out of character demanding justice since the system failed them. Some turn to violence, and others turn to peaceful protests. In my opinion, I don't believe in peaceful protest because protesting has not caused long-lasting change for anyone, especially Black people. When will we learn that change only happens when we change our behavior? This includes apologizing. I have yet to witness an apology that stops the hurt.

This in itself is a form of hope, as hope creates both a positive and negative energy.

All Cultures Are Being Used

I often observe those around me and question people from other countries and their cultures. None of them responded in regard to how Blacks are treated compared to other races. Some even try to defend the way their race treat Black people as a whole, which doesn't surprise me. What *does* surprise me is that some people who look like us claim we are the ones with the problem and we are the ones who have caused unwanted pain in our culture. However, this is a problematic mindset as it makes us vulnerable to whatever bad that could happen by putting our trust in another individual to treat us how they would like to be treated.

Since the United States is a corporation, why are the citizens so against one another? Think about it, business needs us to fund it, nurture it, and cultivate it? Shouldn't we be getting paid for this, apart from the pay we receive from the work we complete? Shouldn't we get paid from the mere fact that our participation in trading, working, and servicing is essential in running this country? We are too busy disagreeing with our own feelings to realize we are being used by the system.

I recall once that I rode down the main highway and saw a group of about five Caucasians standing beside the road with signs. There was one heavy set man with coveralls on, a lady with a long skirt that reached down to her shoes, two younger boys, a girl, and two dogs. I assume they were a family.

The signs read, "Vote for Trump! If you don't like it, go back to where you came from." I couldn't help but look in their direction and shake my head. I desperately wanted to stop to understand what made them feel that Trump was the best candidate. I wanted to deconstruct and challenge their statement, asking them who they were referring to and where those people should go back to? I decided against it though and just drove on.

Clearly, we live in an unfair society. The family who stood with those signs probably make six figures and have a decent insurance plan. To them, Trump is the best candidate because he will serve them and their people. But what about the rest of us? What about minorities? Other races? Those of low status? I can't even imagine what it would be like for everyone to be treated fairly in today's world. Not just African Americans, but Hispanics, Mexicans, Caucasians, and so on. If we change our behaviors and alter our approach to action, then maybe we will all wake up from this nightmare and create change.

Every One Wants To Go To Heaven

Everyone wants to go to heaven, but none wants to die. Isn't that the reality we all avoid? Some have accepted it, while others have yet to do so. Some are too afraid to die because of how they have led their lives. I don't think many people think about the logic of death and why we have to die in the first place. I wonder if people even wonder what happens to our souls, spirits, or the energy we contain when we pass? I often wonder if slave owners thought about the act of murder before committing it. Did they consider its magnitude and the grief it brings? Less not forget about what will happen to them for doing such hateful things to people.

Probably not because if they did, then they wouldn't have done it in the first place. During physical slavery, some were brutally murdered. Imagine being beat so badly to the point of death, or drowning in the ocean to try and escape physical pain. What about being raped until the hurt is intolerable and you accept death? As horrible and unfathomable as these things may sound, they are a reality that our ancestors experienced with little repercussions from perpetrators. That being said, being worked to death doesn't sound as bad in comparison, does it? Let's not forget about the deaths that occurred by those being fed to alligators, or those being burned to death or buried alive. So I ask, which one would you choose if you had a choice: Would you choose to die or would you choose to work until you die?

Religion

How old is religion? According to research, religion is over 2000 years old. Religion can lead all of us to either behave positively or negatively. It is common nature for us to want to assume anything that acknowledges our greatest creation is intended to be good. And so, anything that separates humanity is not good. I believe it's a form of separation. We can all admit that racism has negative impacts on our behaviors and decisions. According to the life we live after physical slavery, religion can be good and bad depending on how the individual chooses to act in accordance with religion. I am in my forties, and throughout my whole life I always felt that something was not right about religion. Now that I am wiser and come to terms I have to think for myself, a lot of religion I was taught was to keep me in control and to do what the government wanted me to do. Well according to the book of romans from the King James Bible, the 13th chapter, it clearly states obey the government and you will not get punished, it also states to obey the laws of the land. Well I can agree to a certain extent because I do feel we should not kill one another, that a justifiable law, but why do the government hire people to go in other countries to kill people. Life after physical slavery has us so dumbed down until some of us volunteer to be physically enslaved still today in 2022. Some feel the 13th amendment abolished slavery. I guess it's all in the way you look at abolishment. To me I feel slavery still exist, and it has multiplied to certain types of slavery. The first type is the working class type. Those are the working class citizens that pay taxes. Then you have the enslaved citizens in the penitentiary. These are the group of people who have to work in the fields or whatever the state require them to do for labor, and the government gets to calls it reform. What exactly are they reforming, because majority of the inmates end up coming back to prison due to not being able to adjust to the society norm due to being so institutionalized. It's a sad reality but this type of stuff has been going on for centuries, and we all can agree that slavery still exist, it's just in a different form. The last type of slavery is the indoctrinated slaves, and that's all of us.

Many different religions divide and separate all of us. Some believe in Allah, Jesus, Jehovah, Buddha, the Pope, Elijah Muhammad, or the Virgin Mary, and so on. Regardless of what religion we choose to follow, we can't argue with the reality that no one will save us from the decisions we make or have made. I grew up a Christian and after 37 years, I decided to start researching religion for myself as I wanted to know why none of my prayers were being answered. I realized it was because I was praying to the wrong energy or God. I realized that I should have been praying to myself because I am the only one that has control over my thoughts, decisions, and actions. I know you might think I'm playing the role of God, but I'm not. Think about it. Our ancestors prayed for freedom from being whipped, raped, and tortured. Still, no one came to their rescue. Sure, in the end they were freed because people helped them and an uprising took place, but many stayed away for fear of being killed during their escape. I can't say I blame those people, either. What would you have done? Would you have tried to escape or would you have stayed and tolerated the abuse? During slavery, Christianity served as a form of hope for many. It was a form of relief and mercy for our people.

I wonder whether or not the slaves ever considered the fact that they worshipped and prayed to the same God as their slave owners. Regardless, I can't help but ask why we still worship a God that feels the need to differentiate between the ways humans get punished. Consider this. Will a slave's soul go to the same heaven as their slave master's? More than that, will slaves still be beaten because they did not obey their earthly master? Let me tell you something you might not want to hear. The God we are worshipping—or *were* worshipping—didn't give a damn about slaves or their wellbeing. Religion is the biggest form of separation in today's society and as humans, we need to abolish it entirely. We need to revert to simply treating one another the same way we'd want others to treat us. If each and every one of us adopt this mentality, then we could never go wrong. We must stop worshipping imaginary figures that were created to give us the illusion of false hope. Abolishing religion in its entirety needs to be done and needs to be attacked as an issue head on. Many people will become antsy at this proposition, but that is simply because our comfort zones are pushing us toward avoidance. I would much rather acknowledge our issues and deal with them if it means change will come for all of us. If our environment isn't good, then none of us can claim to be good. The journey toward change then starts with unlearning bad behaviors. So, we have to acknowledge and convince ourselves that the bad behaviors learned on the plantation were wrong and we can no longer engage in such behavior if we want to see change. There is no miracle that is going to change things for us. Speaking of miracles, do you believe in them?

I don't. To me, miracles are just another form of hope that stems from religion. By believing in miracles, we are believing that things will change and happen without any effort.

Many of us are aware of the story of Jesus. I was. For a long time, I realized that I prayed to someone that I didn't actually know or understand. Like many of you, I was brought up to believe that Jesus was and is our savior. But saved us from what and who? So many people since the start of time have experienced pain, suffering, and trauma. Where was Jesus? Why didn't Jesus do anything when Black people were captured and enslaved? Let's dig a little deeper. According to John 3:16, God supposedly sacrificed His son so that none of us would perish. But so many believers have died and perished. Of course, many argue that this verse in particular is speaking metaphorically rather than literally, but even that can be questioned. We believe the things we're told and taught and don't question whether or not it makes sense. If Jesus is our savior and can save all of us, then why couldn't he save himself? There are so many holes in the story of Jesus when we analyze it. It's safe to conclude that the bible was written for the sins of white people because no other race commits these acts toward others except for white people. And they get away with it, too. Don't get me wrong though, I'm not saying other races and cultures don't cause harm or enslave others, but white people are simply notorious for these behaviors and have historically engaged in such violence the most.

It makes you wonder whether Jesus was a white man. In America, Jesus is depicted as a white man on the cross and this image is spread across all churches, including churches built for Black communities. Why isn't Jesus ever depicted as a Mexican or Indian man?

We have made Jesus a white man because people want to believe that he is superior.

Despite all this, Black people still worship the white savior and will denounce or disown you if you expose these truths. Many people in my own family live and die by Jesus, but Jesus isn't doing anything for them.

Camouflaging Reality

Camouflaging and ignoring the reality of life after slavery is at an all-time high. We are so distracted by commercialized living that we have lost sight of what is real and what makes sense. When I use the word camouflage, I'm using it in the sense that it is something that distracts us from seeing what is real and what is not. Let's address this from a biblical standpoint. First, we're told that life began with Adam and Eve, but this is just based off scripture, as no one can testify to anything otherwise. But if we push the story a little further, we can question how a rib from a man created another life. Next, if creation is a jealous God, why choose to create a man before a woman? Does this not seem selfish or sexist to anyone? We camouflage these concepts by saying that the man is dominant, when in reality, one could be stronger at some things than the other, despite gender. If both individuals were created equally, then it shouldn't matter which one was created first. Then, we camouflage these concepts with death. Who asked Jesus to die for our sins? Why did he have to die if God is all powerful? If I die for someone else's sins, I at least hope it's someone that hasn't done anything to destroy other people.

Next is the story of Noah and the ark. Honestly, this story has more holes in it than a picture used for target practice. I just can't imagine being on a boat with animals without numerous fights occurring. I know I said I don't believe in miracles, but I did at one point. But then, my sister died at the age of one and the illusion of hope and miracles no longer existed in my life.

We all want unity but don't want to take the necessary steps towards creating it. I don't think it will happen in our culture. The only thing we can do is hope it happens, and you know what hope is? It's a waste of energy where no one puts forth any action. Where would we start? I would argue that we should start with abolishing religion, but then again, this could cause more harm than good. It's sad to acknowledge that we live in a society that's too lazy to think for themselves. Getting rid of this laziness is extremely difficult because we have allowed it to go on for generations. Should we start by teaching children and the younger generations in schools?

Or maybe we could start in jails and penitentiaries since the people in there are experiencing pain and suffering. They are locked up trying to survive and protect themselves from the people locked in there with them. Definitely not there I feel it would bring about a bigger up roar than Nat Turners. Speaking of prison, I recently visited a prison and as I pulled up, I observed the scenery, and then observed the inmates behind the bar-wired fences. I listened to the wind and some of the chatter from the inmates. I allowed my spirit to think positively of them and for them. As I left, I noticed a man sitting in a wheelchair behind the fence, away from everyone else. I thought, "It's bad enough to be locked up, but it's even worse to be locked up without being able to move independently and freely." I know many of these individuals have committed crimes that the government deems unlawful, but does it make sense to take away what creation has given all of us? Is this the proper way to punish them? I have never experienced prison, but like so many others, I have been imprisoned mentally. The rules are created by the government, but the government doesn't abide or punish everyone equally.

Imagine Donald Trump and Joe Biden. Two Caucasian men running for president with different agendas, and neither one is advocating for Black people. Regardless of the winner, the race doesn't bring change for an entire race of people living in America. Moreover, neither candidate seems like a great role model. A president should have more than just money to run a country. A president should have morals and respect. African Americans believe that we can be equal in a system that works against us. This is impossible. Both candidates don't know what's really going on in this country from a minority perspective because neither have experienced it. All though old Joe won the seat I still feel things will not be any better and they haven't. As a matter of fact it has gotten worst we are currently in a war, and there are videos exposing the United States government and their old tactics as well as the horrible ways they treat people of color.

Fixing Our Problems

We can't fix all the problems that exist at once. We have to fix them one at a time. No president can be perfect because there is no such thing. People will make mistakes and we must learn from those mistakes to progress. We all experience evil thoughts at some point and some of us carry them out because we have immoral beliefs and a lack of character. So many of us think and feel that because Trump is a racist means he's automatically a bad person. However, I'd choose someone who is straightforward and racist like Trump, over someone who tries to hide their racism like Biden. Biden was responsible for locking up many African Americans, either justly or unjustly. We should all be treated equally because none of us were created equally. Neither candidate is good for society. How did I come to this conclusion? Well, you first have to experience society from all walks of life, not just as an elite player, but as individuals who experience both the good and the bad. Life gives us everything we need, but some of us have inherited more than what we require and our privileges have made it not worth living for others. Nearly every man and woman in congress haven't experienced the way minorities live. The millionaires and billionaires are not making contributions to society to make things better. They give to non-profit organizations that they already own. Life after slavery is chaotic and harmful to the point where many of us can no longer even identify what's good for us or what's bad for us all the way down to our names.

Slave Names and Nick Names

Well this should be interesting. Have you ever thought about your name and where did it come from, especially our last names. A lot of us never question things like this because they were named after someone in their family. Nothing is wrong with that; I think it's cool to be named after our ancestors. Some of our ancestors were warriors and profound people. Their last names and nick names was something totally different. First of all if majority of our people came from Africa, so why do we have European names? Secondly why do we have the same last names as our ancestors slave owners? This type of stuff bothers me because it does pay lineage to our own culture. Next we have our nick names. Some of our nick names came from our character or just our ancestors that has passed on. The nick names were cute until I came across an article talking about slave nick names, and why some slaves had nick names in the first place. Well the ones that stood out the most were mammie and motherfucker. Mammie is a well-known nickname in the black community. As a matter of fact I know 2 people personally that has that nick name. I never told them what their nick name meant in history due to them being called that all their life. From what the article read, Mammie is a slave that nursed, cooked, clean, and sometimes had sex with master. Sounds like a live in mistress if you ask me. I don't think our ancestors really wanted this job, but they had no other choice, just as the men had no other options with buck breaking. Now motherfucking was more derogatory than Mammie. A motherfucker means just what it says; this is a bulk that had sex to repopulate the plantation. Sick if you ask me, but then again was it? It makes you wonder how the earth became repopulated in the first place. Son of a Bitch was another derogatory name. All of these names were very vulgar and offensive to our ancestors just as the word nigger. My ancestors did not know how to read or write so they really didn't know that the nigger is not really a bad name, it's all how a person uses it. Nigger in Greek means black or Negro, as well as a person of color. When the slave owners used the word they would put force behind it causing black people to take the word offensive. Now today our own people use this word towards one another. I assume our ancestors felt they could not get the oppressors to stop, why not join them?

Suffering from the same Disease

We tend to overlook the obvious and fail to realize that we are all going through the same suffering. We are all suffering from not knowing the truth as to what we need to lead a happy and fulfilling life. We were told to follow one religion, but it led us to nothing but unanswered questions and complex misunderstandings of facts until we just assume and continue living our lives. But assuming is just another form of hope. When you assume, you are simply hoping that things play out the way you want or expect. Aren't you all tired of suffering? I know I am. I would much rather be given the playbook to life where everyone is treated fairly. This would allow me to make better decisions. We try to avoid suffering but we still do things that make us suffer like a child told to not do something but we allow curiosity to take over anyways. Life after physical slavery has not changed.

We try things to see how they're going to turn out without thinking about the consequences of our actions. I wish someone would have told our ancestors that they were going to suffer before they made a treaty or trade with other countries. Then the United States or physical slavery wouldn't have even existed. It has been stated that slavery started in what we call Africa but was originally Ethiopia. I don't believe it started that way, though. I think someone became greedy and started it. Why couldn't life go on without these horrible parts of history? I often wonder why evil was created in the first place. I guess it was created to divide us or nourish nature. My husband sometimes tells people when they are searching for a deeper perspective that they must understand why evil exists. He states that evil is only a state of being. Sometimes it's good to look at things differently because it allows your mind to interact with better decisions, which can prevent suffering. Life after physical slavery is hard and it effects everyone. We suffer from the mere fact that we don't know who we are, why we are here, and why we die. Some may say we die because we do not take care of our bodies, or we die from just old age. Well nothing can explain where our spirit comes from or where it goes. After our organs no longer work will our soul meet God, will that be our judgement day or will our spirit live on and go into another baby that is being born? That would explain infinity in life or would it?

Help Our Children

A sad reality in today's society is that children are not being taken care of; they are being abused, beaten, and treated like people were during the physical slavery era. This type of behavior should have been eliminated at the end of slavery, but unfortunately this is not the case. These children have no choice in the matter. They are exposed to bad parenting and I argue that the government helped create this pain. Disrupting individuals' lives plays a part in this because there are broken homes with little to no love for children. Children should be loved and nurtured just like every other human being. Children coming from broken homes where there is no foundation, love, honor, or respect for humankind and it creates a void in them. In 1851, the government created adoption. Some could argue that they were trying to fix a problem they created. I have worked in group homes and if the children are combative, they likely won't be adopted. Imagine being placed for adoption because your parents passed away, made bad decisions, or just no longer want to be parents. Now you have to wait a few years before you will be accepted, and then you finally get adopted by what you thought was a loving family but they end up being a family from hell. You get beaten, molested, and tortured. Of course not all families are like this, but this is a reality of the problem at hand. The only solution to this problem is allowing the white house to be an adoption facility, where there is 24hour surveillance. I know it might sound ridiculous to you but to me I feel give the problem back to the corporation that started it.

Physical enslavement has played a part in this problem. Some say people have to make better decisions with situations they are exposed to. This is much easier said than done. It's a wonderful thing that some children get the opportunity to be adopted into a loving family where they are loved and nurtured. But I also worry for the ones that are adopted and abused. The only way to fix this problem is for children to be placed with an adopted family where they are monitored all the time. Life after physical slavery helped birth this situation. There are also adults that grow up in abusive households. I have come across so many adults that have experienced some of the same upbringing as myself. Some talk about it to heal from it, and others hold on to it as a form of self-destruction and bleed that pain on others.

I once came across a social media post that read, "If you don't heal what hurt you, you will bleed on people that didn't cut you." I can attest to the truth of this statement, as I've experienced it first-hand. Many of us have. Many of us continue to behave in this way and do not recognize that what we are doing is hurting ourselves and those around us. That's why some of the adopted children act out; they don't know what to do with their feelings and emotions. Some act out to keep from being adopted because they are afraid that whatever happened to them will happen again. These children are innocent and if we don't find a solution, abused children will grow into abusive adults.

Who Is Our Enemy

What is an enemy? Google defines an enemy as a person who is actively opposed or hostile to someone or something. This definition can refer to anything and anyone. First, we must look at ourselves and acknowledge ourselves as an enemy because we can cause harm to ourselves. Some may go straight to their past with their thoughts of who and what is their enemy. The enemy today starts with us. We can't change what happened in the past but we can change what will happen to us in the future. Of course, learned behavior plays a part in our demise today. We only respond to the things we feel. However, most times it's not what we are supposed to feel because we are living a lie. Think about the years we've spent eating junk food knowing it was unhealthy.

We didn't consider the fact that we would accumulate high blood pressure, diabetes, kidney failure, or cancer. We started by eating to survive because slave masters only allowed Black people to eat certain things, like leftovers or hog parts that they wouldn't eat. But now we have the opportunity to eat healthy but don't like the acquired taste. I remember growing up and eating whatever was on the table. If I didn't, then I went to bed hungry. We are enemies to ourselves in regard to how we treat one another. Even when we die our family members can die from high blood pressure or diabetes but at the repast we will serve the same food that helped killed the life we was celebrating. I can claim this stemmed from slavery because we don't trust one another to do right by each other. One slave will go against another to gain freedom or recognition from the slave master. This is still going on today.

We will go against our own people to get ahead. However, this type of behavior comes from an individual's pride and it corrupts our way of living as a whole. We are so eager to destroy one another knowing it takes a lot to start over. We sell each other drugs and help destroy families. Then, we get mad at the government for allowing the drugs to be imported from other places. We fail to look at ourselves first. We fail to blame ourselves first. Instead, we blame the government for our downfalls and shortcomings. The rap music industry helped us destroy ourselves, telling our people to rape, kill, and smoke dope because it's the cool thing to do and now today we want to silence it. We are our own enemies.

We have to take accountability for our actions. Just because harmful things are available to us doesn't mean we should engage in them. We have the right to refuse. It's a matter of ignorance. We have access to knowledge to teach us that the things that look familiar and seem normal are in fact causing more harm than good. But we reject the notion because it's easier. Consider the marijuana industry. In our society, marijuana was illegal for a long time. However, in recent years, the marijuana industry has become a big business and is destroying our people. The growers or planters have added chemicals to the herbs to make it even more harmful and addictive for us. They have added colors to make us think it's more potent. We have to get back to our roots and start living from our heritage by engaging in meditation for our mental health, growing our own crops, and hunting our own food. Stop victimizing ourselves because we are our own enemy. We all are.

Organized Crime

We all know it's wrong to rob a bank or to just rob in general. People work hard to accumulate the things they have and then to have it taken from you without you offering it. This is clearly wrong. However, there is a great deal of organized crime in today's society. Let's start by examining history. The number one crime of all crimes was and is slavery. Slavery has evolved to paying taxes today to live or be a person in existence. Next, there are medicines that cause more harm than good. This is a silent crime that doesn't just apply to Black people, but to all of humankind. Consider the COVID-19 pandemic. It has gone on far too long and the government wants everyone to take a vaccine although there is very little proof it will even work. I believe this is a way of instilling fear in all Americans. I personally don't know anyone who has died from COVID-19 but the news is filled with an endless stream of stories claiming that hundreds have lost their lives to the deadly virus. I am not afraid of the virus. Aren't we all going to die anyways? Why worry over something you can't change or control? The pharmaceutical industries are making a living off this pandemic. The sicker and more afraid people are, the more medicine and vaccines are needed. To me, this is considered organized crime. Another organized crime is human trafficking, well wasn't slavery human trafficking? This is the number one organized crime in today's society. In all the states I go through that is all I see on billboards is to stop human trafficking. Where the hell were these billboards 400 hundreds years ago or where was the energy to not even allow it to happen? A lot of people may not think this was an organized crime, but it was, and that was the spice epidemic. There is a type of drug that was called the K2 that was created in a lab or at home where the herbs (K2) were available in convenient stores mostly in the run down areas. This herb was supposed to be a legal drug replacement for marijuana. Well just let's say when a lot of Caucasian children got hooked on it, the government made it illegal. This drug was nothing like the crack epidemic it was worst because people would be talking out of their mind, standing still for hours, running around butt naked and so much more. So now they have made marijuana legal in so many states, when they should have done it that way the first place. Not that I believe or feel any drug that alters your day to day living is bad for you.

Similarly, the government makes laws that they know people will break and imprison them when they do. The spice pandemic was like a bait and switch move. They fine individuals and lock them up and these inmates become victims of even harsher crimes. Then, we have the illegal selling of alcohol. People used to make home brew, moonshine, wine, and any other enhanced substances for the body. This was stopped in 1920 when the government realized that they would make more money legalizing alcohol because the proceeds would go right back into the economy. This also developed into drinking and driving fines. The government always benefits from Americans' poor decisions and it doesn't matter what color or nationality you are. We all have to pay for our own suffering.

Now, the money-making trend is hemp and marijuana. Did you know that marijuana was originally banned to keep white women from being taken advantage of by black men and Mexicans? White women should be offended by such ignorance. Then again, they accept the disrespect and degrading they receive from white men as long as it helps them maintain their status. For example I can remember when I was young probably no more than 7 or 8 years old and I had to go to work with my mom to clean and cook for some white people. Well the wife was very nice so that I could remember, but the husband was fresh and very mean. He would always look at you funny and wink his old stinky eye ate me. I wanted to punch him in it. The wife seemed afraid of him, because she would whisper if she gave us extra food or her hand me down clothes. Sometimes the husband would return home drunk and cursing and we would have to leave early. The next day my mom would have to console the wife because she would be so emotional. I'm sure the husband was abusive to his wife, especially the way she would be acting. The wife would not tell anyone but my mom, probably because she was not working to make money to take care of herself and her children. There were significant number of organized crimes that took place in in history, and no one was able to do anything about it. I think that's where black people learned the analogy what goes on in this house stays in this house.

We still today ignore the consequences for the greater good of ourselves, and society approves of such a behavior and mindset. If we dig further into the concept of organized crime, we can conclude that it includes thieves, drug dealers, military men, abusive husbands, neglectful wives, and of course, the law itself. If the government can't make money off of a crime, then it's considered legal. Let's not forget the crime that occurs in hospices where healthcare workers give narcotics to help ease the pain during death. We tend to think that just because an institution filed for a business name, then they cannot commit crimes. This is not the reality. Crimes should not go against the laws of nature. We have become so accustomed to committing crimes against the universe until it has become a norm for all of us. Life after physical slavery has become so silently brutal. However, we no longer have to be ashamed of it because morals are disregarded and undervalued in society. Last but not lease an organized crime no one really thinks of was and is prostitution. Prostitution became known on the scene in the 1700's when policeman were created. The job policeman was created to outlaw prostitution then it eventually migrated to keep the slaves from running away. In today prostitution is well known in the black community because most black women feel that a man supposed to pay for their sex even if they are married. I think it's stupid and characterless. I am not saying all black women but it is quite a few, feel if a man don't work they don't need him, looking all over the fact of companionship and a father in the household. I feel we need to change this narrative because it shows no form of love to one another.

Christian Home

Consider a Black boy born into poverty. Both of his parents were brought up in a Christian environment. The dad was a police officer and the mom a homemaker. The boy's father was exposed to physical and mental abuse, not to mention neglect and substance abuse. The mom, on the other hand, experienced sexual abuse alongside her mother and siblings. The abuse even manifested to the grandchildren. Evidently, life after slavery was more than just pain. It was a catastrophic act of unwanted behavior. Both parents believed that they had to stay together because they were married regardless of the toxic and abusive behaviors that were going on all because god hates divorce. I have given you the background of a particular family to give you an idea of how it could have started. To me, the son or any child brought up in that family was doomed from the start because of the parents' trauma and suffering. I would also argue that the Christian lifestyle is another form of pain because religion is not part of the culture of these particular people, besides who wants to be abused and knowing it. The young man saw the pain his dad and mom expressed, so he mimic that same type of behavior throughout his life.

This is what life after physical slavery is. It is hoping for things will change, but not doing anything to make a change. We all want what's best for us but never think about whether it would hurt someone else. It's sad to acknowledge that the boy in the scenario above, like many other children in America, didn't even have the opportunity to understand life. Like that little boy, many of us attach ourselves to things that harm us and stunt our growth. We love people that don't love us back. We care for people that don't have our best interests at heart. We put up with abuse in exchange for social status, cars, or money. That boy grew up and followed a path lined with drugs and abuse. He broke laws and was imprisoned. He received no guidance or love from his family or from society. The system continued to destroy his life until he eventually destroyed himself. Some of us are more blessed than others when it comes to receiving nurturing love from family. Some of us never receive it at all.

Dehumanizing the Black Man

Where should we begin? First, look around you. There are more Black men lost in America than there are in any other country. As I have previously mentioned, the foundation of this country was uprooted during the beginning of the slavery era. A Black man is beat down to nothing. A slave is forced to have sex with slave owners—their own mothers—to populate the plantations. Take a large Black man as an example. A man that white people would call a buck. Someone physically strong but mentally weak as a result of all the things he was forced to endure. This type of pain led to emotional turmoil that manifested in all African American males. The Black women saw this and it made her perceive men as inferior. When the Black man tried to take his pride back by joining the military, the women and children were left behind, unprotected.

It's hard to even accept this but when the Black men came back from fighting the white man's war, they were still considered less than human. Note that the Black man also lost his mentality and wellbeing after returning from war. Some white people today still adopt this mentality. They still view Black men and Black people as inferior and subhuman. Even if the Black man tried to recreate his foundation, the Black woman has become sufficient enough to not need their support except in regard to procreation, and even then a lot of black men are not needed due to Dr. Crappy Rotham created a sperm bank in 1977 to help with that it was first created in Tokyo Japan. Black women today are independent and self-sufficient. Still, Black men and their nurturing mechanisms were desperately needed in the Black homes and are needed today. However, after years of being rejected by the Black women and feeling unnecessary, the Black men turned to white women for acceptance.

None of this is to say that I care who you love. This is simply to say that if who you love harms the greater good of the Black foundation, then it's problematic for the entire Black community. Moreover, the Black man was dehumanized through what is known as the Vacancy Act. This act prohibited Black men from working after they returned from war. According to the encyclopedia of Virginia, the Vacancy Act took place as the Vagrancy Act of 1866, passed by the General Assembly on January 15, 1866, forced into employment, for a term of up to three months, any person who appeared to be unemployed or homeless. If so-called vagrants ran away and were recaptured, they would be forced to work for no compensation while wearing balls and chains. More formally known as the Act Providing for the Punishment of Vagrants, the law came shortly after the American Civil War (1861–1865), when hundreds of thousands of African Americans, many of them just freed from slavery, wandered in search of work and displaced family members. As such, the act criminalized freed people attempting to rebuild their lives and perhaps was intended to contradict Governor Francis H. Pierpont's public statement discouraging punitive legislation. Shortly after its passage, the commanding general in Virginia, Alfred H. Terry, issued a proclamation declaring that the law would reinstitute "slavery in all but its name" and forbidding its enforcement.

Proponents argued that the law applied to all people regardless of race, but the resulting controversy, along with other southern laws restricting African American rights, helped lead to military rule in the former Confederacy and congressional Reconstruction. It is unknown to what degree it was ever enforced, but the Vagrancy Act remained law in Virginia until 1904. Black men were captured, locked up, and couldn't escape. This is similar to today's prison systems where Black men are caged like animals. Of course, all nationalities are also affected by this. However, Black men don't become criminals by just deciding to be criminals. They do it by being exposed to criminal behavior or as a result of not being self-sufficient. Most times it's because someone close to them encouraged their decisions. I'm sure a lot of people in the Black community can relate. Black men are scared by white men. There is no profound help for the Black man from the government. Once you realize this, you may develop more sympathy for these men.

Now, the Black man is addicted to drugs and white women and have no clue where he fits in society. Black men have feelings, but society wants to treat them as though they are not allowed to express or even feel any emotions. Taking a look even deeper, there is no profound help for the black man in America. Even if a black man becomes a single father and needs assistance the social economics gives them the third wheel response, some places they can't even get public housing assistance. This is sad why not help all humans the same? It's time for us to change this negative narrative and help rehabilitate the issues we helped create.

Paradise after It All

What is paradise if you never experienced it? We all could only imagine it. To me paradise is the ultimate place of no worries. Some people imagine it as a place of illustration from the Garden of Eden, the metaphoric way of where Adam and Eve supposed to have been introduced into the world. Well life after slavery is not what we can ever imagine. This is something that never should have existed in the first place. We have to make up our own paradise, and what we would desire for it to be within limits. There will always be worries in this life, because no one knows why or who created us. What would be paradise for you may not be paradise for the next person. Paradise for me would be to exist without questions. That is the only way to eliminate worries. Everyone wants paradise, but we will not come together to create it, maybe because paradise is just a figure of speech, or maybe because paradise is untouchable. It would be nice to live without worries don't you think? Then complaints will not exist. Time after time I believe a lot of our ancestors and some of the people that are living today allowed this to cross their minds maybe once or twice. Especially when you have the moment in life to elevate everything that is not of us. Simplicity can't exist in a world of different views of what we all desire to be the most important manifestation we could ever experience. This type of paradise should exist where there is no worries, doubts, or regrets, and last but not lease no harm. There should be no harm to any man kind that goes for all nations, even the animals, although that would mean life could not reciprocate. . Maybe we really have to have death in order to have life. Maybe that is paradise and that is to reincarnate back into life.

The Conclusion

This isn't really the end, but I will end the conversation here for now. This book tells you about most of the illusions of life after physical slavery. This book exposes most of the metaphors that were hidden from society. People think their way of living was derived from honesty, but have lost the reality of it all. They have lost sight of the politics, the self-hate, and the demoralizing of creation. Life after physical slavery never ended because we are all very much enslaved to the lies we have been fed for too long. We have lost our morals because we don't know what love really means.

Some may dismiss the writings in this book, but nevertheless, these writings are someone's truth.

Why should we remember the past? Because we can't have a future without it.

People believe that changing the minds of individuals is not possible. However, it is actually the truth that can't be changed. Belief is just an illusion.

I dare you to read more on this topic and comprehend the truth of the reality we are all living in. We all want happiness and love. We all want to live life without suffering and pain—myself included. I don't want to pass on the pain and trauma I've received from previous generations onto my own children. This cycle has to stop. As John Henry Clarke profoundly wrote, "Powerful people cannot afford to educate the people that they oppress, because once you are truly educated, you will not ask for power." Taking things one day at a time helps us educate ourselves and acknowledge our reality. However, we must first separate our reality from others. Clarke also wrote, "Whoever is in control of the hell in your life, is your devil." Spirits never die, only our outer shell does. The future only exists because of past creation.

Printed in the United States
by Baker & Taylor Publisher Services